W9-CHE-171

SHARK

Written by Simon Mugford

an imprint of
■SCHOLASTIC
www.scholastic.com

Scholastic and Tangerine Press and associated logos are trademarks of Scholastic Inc.
Published by Tangerine Press, an imprint of Scholastic Inc., 557 Broadway, New York, NY 10012
0-439-68102-2
Printed and bound in China

24 Contents

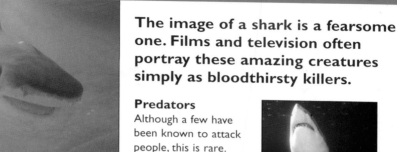

Kings of the Deep

The image of a shark is a fearsome one. Films and television often portray these amazing creatures simply as bloodthirsty killers.

Predators

Although a few have been known to attack people, this is rare. Every year, far more humans are attacked by domestic pets than by sharks.

Great white shark.

Super Species

About 375 shark species exist, ranging in size from the dwarf dogfish at 6.5 in. (16 cm) long to the whale shark at about 39 ft. (12 m) long.

Elasmobranch

Although they do not look alike, sharks are closely related to manta rays, skates, guitarfish, and sawfish. Together, these are known as the elasmobranch family.

Manta ray.

Not all sharks are dangerous.

Harmless
Some sharks are fierce hunters, but they are doing what comes naturally. And many species are harmless, like the nurse shark.

Fish
A shark is a type of fish. Many different species of sharks exist in many shapes and sizes.

Flexible Friend
The main difference between sharks and other fish is that their skeletons are flexible, not hard and bony.

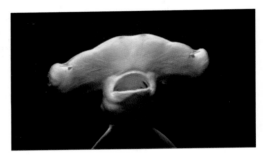

With its wide set eyes, the hammerhead shark is able to see for great distances.

Torpedo
Many sharks have a torpedo-shaped body— excellent for swimming at great speeds. Some living on the bottom of the ocean are rounder and heavier.

Swim Bladder
Bony fish also have a swim bladder—a kind of sack that they inflate and deflate to move up or down in the water. Sharks do not have these and most need to keep moving so they do not sink.

Spots and Stripes

Sharks vary in color, ranging from reddish brown and metallic blue to gray or almost black. Many have markings such as spots or stripes. Shark skin does not have scales like bony fish, but is covered with small, toothlike denticles. The skin is very rough.

The markings on the lesser spotted dogfish help to camouflage it against the sea bed.

Traveling Sharks

Different species of sharks are found all over the world, in coastal areas and deep ocean. Some travel many thousands of miles, and others stay in a small area.

Still Learning

Sharks are fascinating and mysterious creatures, and our knowledge about them is limited.

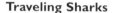

The gray reef shark is torpedo-shaped, meaning it can swim through the water at great speeds.

Sharks vary greatly in appearance, size, and color, but some features are common to most species.

Huge mouth

Most sharks have several rows of very sharp teeth to tear up food.

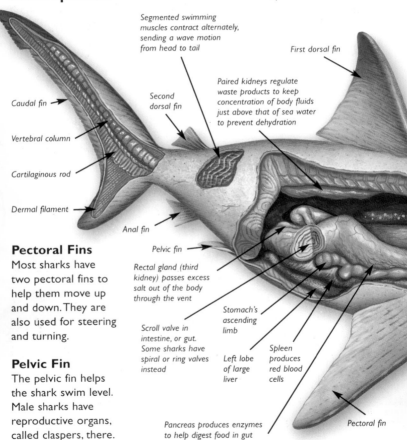

Segmented swimming muscles contract alternately, sending a wave motion from head to tail

First dorsal fin

Second dorsal fin

Paired kidneys regulate waste products to keep concentration of body fluids just above that of sea water to prevent dehydration

Caudal fin

Vertebral column

Cartilaginous rod

Dermal filament

Anal fin

Pelvic fin

Rectal gland (third kidney) passes excess salt out of the body through the vent

Scroll valve in intestine, or gut. Some sharks have spiral or ring valves instead

Stomach's ascending limb

Left lobe of large liver

Spleen produces red blood cells

Pancreas produces enzymes to help digest food in gut

Pectoral fin

Pectoral Fins

Most sharks have two pectoral fins to help them move up and down. They are also used for steering and turning.

Pelvic Fin

The pelvic fin helps the shark swim level. Male sharks have reproductive organs, called claspers, there.

Caudal Fin
This is what most sharks use to propel themselves through the water.

Dorsal Fin
Most sharks have two dorsal fins. These fins help a shark stay upright. The rear is usually smaller.

Viviparous Sharks
Viviparous sharks give birth to up to 100 live young called pups.

Oviparous Sharks
Oviparous sharks lay eggs that attach to rocks. They hatch after six to 15 months.

Ovoviviparous Sharks
Ovoviviparous sharks grow in an egg inside the female's body. The young shark hatches while it is still inside the female's body.

The leathery shell of an oviparous shark's egg lies entangled among sea plants.

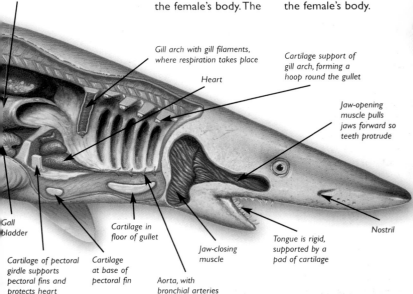

Stomach's descending limb

Gill arch with gill filaments, where respiration takes place

Heart

Cartilage support of gill arch, forming a hoop round the gullet

Jaw-opening muscle pulls jaws forward so teeth protrude

Gall bladder

Cartilage in floor of gullet

Jaw-closing muscle

Tongue is rigid, supported by a pad of cartilage

Nostril

Cartilage of pectoral girdle supports pectoral fins and protects heart

Cartilage at base of pectoral fin

Aorta, with bronchial arteries

Sharks can see, hear, smell, taste, and touch things like us. However, they are specially adapted for the underwater world so that they can find their way around, communicate, and find food.

Smell

A shark's sense of smell is its most useful and highly developed sense. Sharks can detect weak smells in huge amounts of water.

Vision

Sharks' eyes are sensitive to light and can find some things in very dark, murky water.

The great white's ampullae of Lorenzini (sensory organs to detect the electric field of its prey) are particularly prominent.

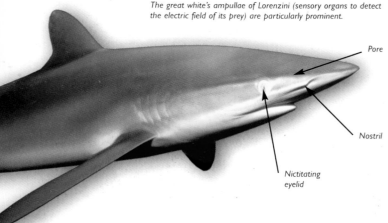

Pore

Nostril

Nictitating eyelid

The red line indicates the shark's lateral line system, which alerts the shark to prey and predators.

Sixth Sense

Sharks also have a sixth sense. They have special pores on their heads called ampullae of Lorenzini. These pick up very weak electrical signals produced by the muscles of living things in the water.

Bio Compass

It is thought that sharks that travel thousands of miles use this sense to tune in to the Earth's magnetic field. This biological compass helps them find their way around the oceans.

Sound

Sharks can detect sound waves and movement in the water thanks to the system of nerves along their sides.

Touch

They can feel things with their nose. Some have barbels (feelers) that they use to find things buried in the sea bottom.

Taste

Their taste buds are on bumps inside the mouth. They will spit out anything they don't find tasty.

The barbels on a nurse shark help it find food.

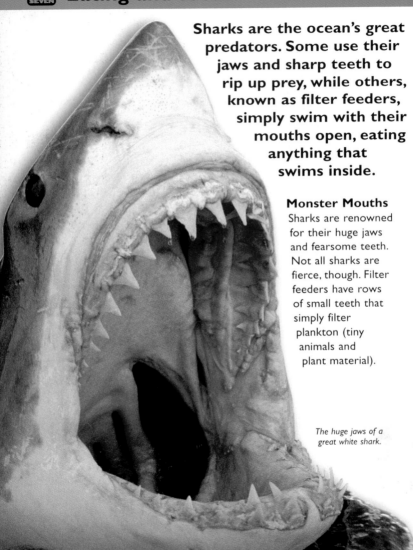

Sharks are the ocean's great predators. Some use their jaws and sharp teeth to rip up prey, while others, known as filter feeders, simply swim with their mouths open, eating anything that swims inside.

Monster Mouths

Sharks are renowned for their huge jaws and fearsome teeth. Not all sharks are fierce, though. Filter feeders have rows of small teeth that simply filter plankton (tiny animals and plant material).

The huge jaws of a great white shark.

A tiger shark feeds on the carcass of a sperm whale.

typically have several rows of teeth—some sharks can have thousands of teeth at one time—and a new tooth simply rotates into place. Also, the teeth get bigger as the shark grows. Some sharks may grow, lose, and replace as many as 30,000 teeth in a lifetime.

Tooth Talk

One thing common among all sharks is that as their teeth wear out, they are replaced by new ones. Sharks

Different Teeth

Sharks' teeth vary by species, depending on what they eat. Sharks that eat slippery fish like squid have long, curved teeth. Serrated teeth are good for cutting up bony fish.

The fearsome teeth of the tiger shark. Note also the shark's prominent ampullae of Lorenzini.

Tooth Types

Spiked teeth grip small prey as the shark tears it apart. Flat, strong teeth are used to crush and crunch up tough shellfish.

Strong Jaw

Some sharks have a combination of different types of teeth. The tiger shark will eat almost anything and has a wide variety of teeth. Its teeth and jaws are strong enough to cut through a turtle shell!

The different types of teeth found in sharks.

Sharks first swam in the oceans more than 300 million years ago —long before dinosaurs walked the Earth.

The fearsome megalodon is thought to have been able to eat creatures as large as whales.

Mighty Molars

We only know about the megalodon because scientists found and have been able to study its fossilized teeth.

The fossilized tooth of a megalodon.

Megalodon

Megalodon was an enormous shark. Scientists estimate that it grew to more than 39 ft. (12 m) long —more than twice the size of its present-day relative, the great white (see pages 32-33). It is not known exactly when megalodon became extinct, but it could have lived as recently as 12,000 years ago.

Huge Jaw

Fossilized megalodon teeth up to 6.75 in. (17 cm) long have been found in Europe, India, Australia, and both North and South America. The size of the teeth suggests that its jaws could open to about 6 ft. (1.8 m) wide and about 7 ft. (2 m) high.

The huge fossilized jaw of a megalodon.

Hundreds of Teeth

Megalodon probably had hundreds of teeth at any one time, which it used to bite large chunks out of its prey. It probably ate other large creatures such as whales.

Great White Shark

No other megalodon remains have been found (shark skeletons do not preserve well), but most scientists believe it was a bigger,

slimmer version of the great white shark.

The megalodon existed at the same time as the helicoprion (pictured above), which was thought to have had a spiral-toothed mouth.

Blue Shark

The sleek and graceful blue shark is one of the fastest swimmers and a genuine globetrotter. They are found all over the world, from Australia and South Africa to the coasts of North America and the United Kingdom.

Channel Swimmer

The blue sharks of the Atlantic migrate across the oceans each year, following the warm currents of the Gulf Stream up to Europe.

Right: Blue sharks like to eat squid.

Left: The blue shark's long, slim body and snout make it an elegant and powerful swimmer.

Squid Eaters

Their diet consists mostly of squid. Their pointed, serrated teeth are well-suited to handle the slippery, rubbery flesh of their prey.

The streamlined blue shark moves swiftly through the water.

Powerful Swimmer

The blue shark's long, slim body and extra-long caudal fin (the tail) make it a very powerful and elegant swimmer.

A blue shark being tagged by a diver.

FAST FACTS

Location
Worldwide

Habitat
Open water

Size
12.5 ft. (3.8 m)

Fact
The blue shark is endangered because of overfishing.

The strangely shaped head of the hammerhead shark makes it the most distinctive of all shark species. The nine subspecies of hammerhead come in a wide range of sizes and color.

The hammerhead's large eyes provide it with excellent vision.

Great Hammerhead

The largest of all the hammerhead sharks—the great hammerhead—is an extremely menacing predator with a very good sense of smell. It will eat any other fish, squid, octopus, and shellfish, but its favorite meal is the stingray. It attacks the ray by holding it down with its hammer and taking bites out of its wings.

Hammerheads are among the most ferocious of all sharks and have been known to attack people.

A diver observing a hammerhead shark eating jackfish.

Use Your Head

Experts have yet to discover a reason for this shark's unusual head. However, with the eyes positioned at either end of the hammer, they can spot their prey very easily. The shape of the head also provides extra lift, much like the wings of an aircraft, as it swims through the water.

The hammerhead shark is one of the oddest-looking creatures of the sea.

Sixth Sense

Like all sharks, the hammerhead has the sixth sense that allows it to detect weak electrical signals emitted by other sea creatures. The hammerhead has a large number of ampullae of Lorenzini (see page 9) on the sides of its head, which pick up these signals and help it find and catch its prey. Combined with its unusual eyes, the hammerhead is a well-equipped hunter.

FAST FACTS

Location
Worldwide, but mostly tropical areas

Habitat
Warm coastal waters

Size
Up to 20 ft. (6 m)

Fact
They eat members of their own species!

Makos are the fastest-swimming sharks and are known to leap right out of the water.

Fast Swimmers

Scientists have found it difficult to measure the speed of makos, but it is estimated that they can swim up to 25 mph (40 km/h). Some have even suggested that they can reach 60 mph (97 km/h)!

Fast Fish

Mako sharks are similar in many ways to another of the world's fastest fish, the tuna. Like tuna, mako sharks make a popular catch for fishermen around the world.

An Even Keel

To reach such speeds, makos have a caudal fin that helps them move through the water. They also have a keel on their undersides to help them change direction.

Gulp!

The mako's speed allows it to catch other fast fish, such as tuna, mackerel, and swordfish.

The streamlined body of the mako shark.

A mako catches up with its prey, bites it hard, and swallows it in one gulp. Makos have been known to swallow fish that are about one-sixth of their own body weight.

In Deep Water

Makos prefer deep, cool waters and in the warm Pacific Ocean. They can be found at depths of 650 to 1,300 ft. (200 to 400 m). On the rare occasions that they come near shore, they pose a threat to people.

Motoring Along

Mako sharks are so fast, they can easily keep up with a motorboat!

FAST FACTS

Location
Temperate and tropical seas

Habitat
Deep ocean waters

Size
Up to 12 ft. (3.7 m)

Fact
Known as bonito or blue pointer.

Above: A jaw of a mako shark, with its variety of teeth types.

Left: Its caudal fin helps the mako shark move quickly.

As its name suggests, the tiger shark is one of the most fearsome sharks in the ocean.

Terrible Teeth

It has razor-sharp, serrated teeth and can grow to an equally intimidating size.

Good Sense

Like many killer sharks, tigers have extremely sharp senses. They can detect electric currents in the water, have very good eyesight, and a keen sense of smell. A special gill, called a spinacle, behind its eyes helps a tiger shark's senses by allowing oxygen to flow to the eyes and brain.

FAST FACTS

Location
Worldwide, but mainly tropical seas

Habitat
Open coastal waters

Size
Up to 20 ft. (6 m)

Fact
One of the most feared sharks.

Tiger sharks hunt just below the water's surface, and so they are often responsible for attacks on people.

Anything Goes

Tiger sharks are well-known for not being fussy eaters. Hunting just beneath the water's surface, they will eat anything, from fish, turtles, and other sharks to crabs, shellfish, jellyfish, and sea birds. Tiger sharks have even been known to eat junk food like cans and tires!

Tiger sharks often hunt in groups (above), and have been known to eat garbage (below).

Stripes and Spots

The tiger shark gets its name from the striped markings on its back, rather than from its ferocious reputation. Young tiger sharks have spots, which grow together to form stripes as they mature.

A tiger shark feeding on a marlin carcass.

Thresher sharks come in three varieties —the common thresher, the pelagic thresher, and the bigeye thresher.

The large eyes of the thresher shark help it seek out prey.

is a very powerful swimmer and is threatened by overfishing.

it with a very fast blow from its tail. Dinner is then easy to swallow!

Long Tail
Their distinctive feature is an extremely long caudal fin. The upper part is as long as its body! Like the mako shark (pages 18-19), it

Stunned to Death
The thresher shark gets its name from the way it uses its tail. To catch and eat its prey, the thresher approaches it and stuns or even kills

Lunch is Served
Threshers will sometimes hunt in groups, circling large numbers of fish to get an easy meal.

The thresher shark's tail can stun or kill its prey.

Threshers often swim close to the surface, making them a popular catch for sports fishermen.

Killing Power

The killing power of its tail means that it does not need very large teeth and jaws. Of course, being a shark, its teeth are still sharp!

Popular Catch

Thresher sharks are a popular catch for fishermen, but they are hard to handle once caught. Their tails are known to have caused serious injuries as the sharks are pulled onto the boat.

Not Aggressive

Threshers are not aggressive toward people, though divers still need to be careful around them.

Heavy Babies

The thresher shark gives birth to fewer pups than other sharks (between two and six).

The average length of a thresher shark at birth is 5 ft. (1.5 m).

FAST FACTS

Location
Tropical oceans

Habitat
Open coastal waters

Size
16 to 20 ft. (5 to 6 m)

Fact
They are nocturnal.

Whale Shark

As its name suggests, the whale shark is very big. In fact, it's the biggest shark (and the biggest fish) in the world!

A whale shark being studied by a diving researcher.

FAST FACTS

Location
Warm oceans

Habitat
Open coastal waters

Size
Up to 59 ft. (18 m)

Fact
They swim by moving their whole bodies, not just their tails.

Big Beasts
Adult whale sharks are huge. The smallest are 39 ft. (12 m) long, and they can weigh 14.5 tons (13.2 tonnes).

Gentle Giants
Such a large shark may sound scary, but whale sharks are not at all dangerous; they are true gentle giants. They don't seem to mind if people get too close, and divers have even ridden on their backs!

Big Mouth
As you would expect, a really big shark like the whale shark has a very big mouth.

The big and beautiful whale shark has a mouth measuring up to 4.5 ft (1.4 m) wide.

Measuring up to 4.5 ft. (1.4 m) wide, its mouth is at the very front of its head, rather than underneath, like most other sharks.

Tiny Teeth

Whale sharks have around 3,000 teeth, but they are all very tiny and not used very much. This is because the whale shark is a filter feeder (see page 10). They feed by swimming with their mouths open, taking in huge amounts of seawater and any small creatures.

Open Wide... Swallow

The gill slits at the back of its head work like a sieve, letting out water but trapping food in the mouth. When it has a large mouthful of food, it swallows. Whale sharks eat a lot of plankton as well as other small fish.

Whale sharks swim with their mouths wide open, sifting the ocean for plankton.

Although they are not really sharks, rays are very closely related. The largest of all is the manta ray—a scary-looking fish, but in reality, one of the gentlest of sea creatures.

The manta ray is a filter feeder, waiting for food to swim into its jaws.

Devilfish

Fishermen and sailors once thought that the manta ray would swallow boats and people whole. The manta's enormous size and the two "horns" sticking from the front of its head led to the misnomer devilfish, or devil ray.

The underbelly of the body is mainly white to hide the manta ray from predators lurking below.

Toothless

In fact, mantas are harmless filter feeders. They have no teeth and use their "horns"— types of fins—to funnel plankton into their mouths as they swim along the ocean floor.

Manta Rays

Aquatic Acrobat

To see a manta ray swimming is an incredible sight. They use their wings (types of pectoral fins) to fly through the water. Despite their enormous size, manta rays are quite acrobatic and can sometimes be seen leaping out of the ocean. In fact, they have been known to leap 14.75 ft. (4.5 m) out of the water!

Peaceful

Manta rays have few predators. From a young age, they learn to hide themselves by sitting on the sea floor and covering themselves with sand. Even fishermen are not interested in manta rays, so they have a peaceful life!

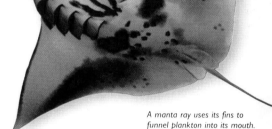

A manta ray uses its fins to funnel plankton into its mouth.

Manta rays are spectacular to watch.

FAST FACTS

Location
Tropical oceans

Habitat
Open coastal waters

Size
Up to 29.5 ft. (9 m)

Fact
Also known as the devilfish, or devil ray.

The basking shark is the second-largest fish in the world, after the whale shark. Basking sharks get their name because they spend most of their time near the surface, basking in sunshine.

Cruise Control
In fact, basking sharks are more likely at the surface looking for food. Like whale sharks, they are filter feeders—cruising around with their mouths open and taking in huge quantities

Basking sharks love swimming near the surface of the water.

of water and plankton. Basking sharks can process up to 400,000 gallons (1.5 million liters) of water an hour!

Deep Sleep
They spend the colder parts of the year on the sea floor, though nobody is quite sure why. Some scientists think that they could be in hibernation.

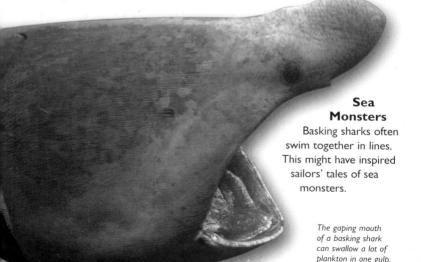

Sea Monsters
Basking sharks often swim together in lines. This might have inspired sailors' tales of sea monsters.

The gaping mouth of a basking shark can swallow a lot of plankton in one gulp.

The fin of a basking shark is often used in food products.

Basking sharks can reach up to 33 ft. (10 m) in length.

Britain and Ireland. Their fins are used to make shark-fin soup and their livers, which can make up a quarter of the shark's weight, are used for oil.

Rough Skin

Basking sharks spend a lot of time close to the shore, either alone or in large groups. They are often seen by people and are not at all dangerous. Their skin however, is very rough and can injure swimmers.

Shark-fin Soup

Basking sharks are fished wherever they are found, including around the coasts of

FAST FACTS
Location
Temperate waters
Habitat
Coastal areas, near the water's surface
Size
Up to 33 ft. (10 m)
Fact
Its closest relative is the great white.

You are most likely to find the white tip reef shark around **Pacific Ocean coral reefs,** such as those off the coast of **Australia.**

White Tips
White tips are quite small, slender, and dark gray in color. The dorsal fin and caudal fin have white tips. That is where this shark's name comes from.

White tips hiding under a rock.

Standing Still
During the day, white tips spend their time in sea caves or similar places in a coral reef.

White tips swim around the sea floor at night looking for food.

30

White tips spend a lot of time in caves, looking for food.

In a large cave, many white tips will gather together, stacked on top of one another. They may remain perfectly still on the ocean bottom for long periods of time.

Night Lovers

White tips are most active at night, when they swim around the reefs or sea floor searching for food.

They are excellent at finding food in holes, under ledges, and in other hideaways.

Rarely Aggressive

They stay in the same area for months or years. Despite this, they do not guard their territory and are very rarely aggressive. They will often take food offered to them by divers.

FAST FACTS

Location
Tropical waters

Habitat
Ocean bottom in coastal areas, near coral reefs

Size
Up to 7 ft. (2.1 m)

Fact
Often on the ocean floor looking for food.

Great White Shark

Probably the most famous and feared of all sharks, the great white is the ocean's most ferocious predator.

Feared and Ferocious

Despite being so well known, great whites are rarely seen, and they are not yet fully understood.

Big Appetite

Great whites will eat pretty much anything they can get their jaws on. Their preferred meals are large fish, other sharks, sea birds, seals, and sea lions— anything that's big enough to satisfy their large appetite.

Man-eater

They have been known to attack people, but thankfully, this is rare. It is thought that a great white can go without food for up to two months after a big meal.

Terrible Teeth

This fearsome fish is well-equipped for hunting. The great white has around 3,000 teeth at any one time. They are triangular, serrated, razor-sharp, and up to 5 in. (7.5 cm) long.

The nose is made of cartilage, which is less fragile than bone and can withstand damage.

Great White Shark

The white belly of the great white helps it blend in with the sky above.

Fast Swimmer

The great white's streamlined shape and pointed snout make it a fast swimmer for a shark of its size. They can swim up to 15 mph (24 km/h).

A great white shark attacks a Cape fur seal, by butting it from underneath.

Camouflaged

Only the great white's underbelly is white—it's gray on top. This makes it very hard to spot from below, and makes it easier for them to sneak up on their prey.

Hunting Prey

Great whites have very sensitive ampullae of Lorenzini to detect electrical currents in the water. They also have a great sense of smell. They can detect one drop of blood in 1.2 million gallons (4.6 million liters) of water.

Great whites often attack the protective cages of diving researchers.

FAST FACTS

Location
Temperate waters

Habitat
Coastal areas

Size
Up to 23 ft. (7 m)

Fact
It was made famous by the movie "Jaws."

Several types of dogfish shark roam the seas. Relatively small, dogfish are the most common shark in the world. They are often caught and used by people for food and oil.

The skin of a dogfish is rough and spiny.

food on the sea bottom. The spines contain a mild poison, which can cause a nasty wound.

Traveling Band

They are called dogfish because they travel and hunt in large schools. These groups are often made up of dogfish of the same age or sex, and they

Poisonous Spines

The spiny dogfish is the most common of all. It is gray with white spots and is known for the sharp spines on its back. These are used to protect it from predators as it spends its time searching for

Dogfish are well-camouflaged. Their colors hide them amid the plants and rocks of the ocean.

can sometimes contain thousands of individuals.

Tiny Baby

Baby dogfish are tiny, rarely reaching more than 4 ft. (1.2 m) in length.

A greater spotted dogfish looking for food.

FAST FACTS

Location
Temperate waters

Habitat
Coastal areas

Size
Up to 4 ft. (1.2 m)

Fact
The most common type of shark.

Look out for those poisonous spines!

Shark Sandwich

As the most common type of shark, it is also the one that is most eaten by people. In Britain, it is called rock salmon. The fish and chips so commonly eaten there are more likely dogfish and chips!

No one is sure how nurse sharks came by their name, but they do make a sucking sound like a baby!

The nurse shark has barbels to help it locate potential prey.

are shaped like a fan and are designed to crush the hard shells of the prey that it eats.

Smooth Skin

Nurse sharks are a dark gray-brown and sometimes have spots. Unlike many sharks, a nurse shark's skin is smooth to the touch. They have a wide head and very strong jaws.

Social Sharks

Nurse sharks are large, slow-moving, and known as one of the most social of all sharks because they are always in groups.

Fan Teeth

They live mainly on the sea bottom, where they feed on shrimp, lobster, crabs, and any other shellfish. The nurse shark's teeth

Whiskers

The most distinctive thing about a nurse shark's appearance is the two whiskerlike

Nurse sharks usually live on the sea bottom, feeding on the creatures which live there.

It's possible for divers to get very close to nurse sharks.

barbels on its lower jaw. These thin, fleshy organs help them touch and taste food.

Nursing School

As well as living together in large schools, nurse sharks generally stay in the same area. During the day, they will stay together on the sea bottom, piled up on top of one another.

Captive

Nurse sharks do well in captivity, so you may see one up close if you visit an aquarium or marine park.

FAST FACTS

Location
Warm, shallow waters

Habitat
Near coasts, reefs, and mudflats

Size
Up to 14 ft. (4.25 m)

Fact
A distant relative of the whale shark.

Nurse sharks are slow-moving and graceful.

The leopard shark is so named because of its markings —dark brown spots on a silver background.

A leopard shark blends in well with the rocky sea bed.

Camouflage

The leopard shark changes its skin color to adapt to its environment. This helps it hide in coral— a good source of food —and rock. When a shark dies, its body decomposes to form coral for the next generations.

Diet

The leopard shark lives on a diet of worms, clams, crabs, shrimps, octopus, and other small fish found at the bottom of the sea. It uses its sharp teeth to capture these animals.

The leopard shark lies in wait for prey while resting on the ocean floor.

The skin of a leopard shark looks scaly, very much like that of a fish.

Babies

The female leopard shark produces an egg, which is kept inside the body. When the egg hatches, the shark gives birth. She can give birth to as many as 30 pups in one litter. An animal that reproduces in this way is called ovoviviparous (see page 7).

Age

The leopard shark lives to be about 30 years old. Males reach adulthood between the ages of 7 and 13, and females between 10 and 15.

FAST FACTS

Location
Pacific Coast

Habitat
Bays, near the shore

Size
Up to 6.5 ft. (2 m)

Fact
Very shy and not considered a threat to humans.

A distinctively marked leopard shark.

The megamouth was discovered when one was found tangled up with the anchor of a naval ship.

Discovery

The first megamouth was discovered in 1976 off the coast of Hawaii. Since the discovery, scientists have struggled to find out more about these fascinating creatures.

The megamouth can grow to 16.5 ft. (5 m) long.

Slow Movers

The big megamouth is slow-moving, and it is thought that they do not travel great distances.

Rubber Lips

The megamouth's body is rounded. With thick, rubbery lips and widely spaced eyes on a very large head (almost as long as the main part of its body), it is certainly an unusual-looking creature.

The huge mouth of the megamouth shark is rarely photographed.

Big Mouth

The most distinctive feature of the megamouth shark is its mouth, which is ... well, megabig! At up to 3.25 ft. (1 m) across, it uses this huge mouth to scoop up large amounts of plankton and other small creatures near the surface at night.

Glowing Lips

Only a few megamouths have been found, and very little is known about them. Scientists

The megamouth's glowing lips.

don't agree about its glowing lips. Some say the megamouth uses them to attract larger prey; others think that its mouth reflects light from its luminous prey.

More Mystery

With the sea largely unexplored, other mysterious creatures may be lurking in the oceans.

FAST FACTS

Location
Warm oceans

Habitat
Deep sea areas

Size
Up to 16.5 ft. (5 m)

Fact
First discovered off the coast of Hawaii in 1976.

The deep yellow color along the back of the lemon shark helps to explain its name. It is one of the most studied sharks in the world.

Attracted to Color

Lemon sharks are commonly found near the water surface in bays, docks, and river mouths. They have been known to attack people if disturbed or provoked, and it is thought that they

A lemon shark being studied.

could be attracted to the bright colors of swimwear and safety equipment.

Easy to Study

Despite this, many have been brought into captivity and studied by scientists. Unlike many shark species, lemon sharks do not need to keep swimming to breathe, which makes them fairly easy to study.

Shake

All sharks shed their teeth and grow new ones, but lemon sharks do it more often than any other, gaining a

A diver takes a close look at a lemon shark.

Young lemon sharks out on the prowl.

The lemon shark has a very streamlined shape.

new set every seven to eight days! Its teeth are long, thin, and very sharp. Upon catching its prey, the shark shakes its head very quickly to cut it up.

Hideaway

When lemon sharks are young, they stay close to the area in which they were born, hiding from predators and feeding on fish. With age, they move farther offshore.

FAST FACTS

Location
Warm oceans

Habitat
Coastal areas

Size
Up to 10 ft. (3 m)

Fact
Most common off the coast of Florida.

As their name suggests, bull sharks are large, aggressive, and are thought to attack people quite often. However, they do not have horns!

Fresh Water

Bull sharks are very common in the world's warm tropical oceans and spend a lot of time close to the shore. They are also able to survive for

Bull sharks may be sensitive to low-frequency sounds created by movement.

long periods of time in fresh water. Because of this, they are common visitors to estuaries, rivers, and lakes.

FAST FACTS

Location
Warm oceans

Habitat
Coastal areas

Size
Up to 11.5 ft. (3.5 m)

Fact
One of the most dangerous sharks in the world.

Traveling Far

Bull sharks have been found as far as 1,750 mi. (2,800 km) up the Mississippi River and 2,485 mi. (4,000 km) up the Amazon River in Peru. They have also been seen in inland lakes in Africa and South America.

Bull sharks have been sighted as far apart as the Mississippi and Amazon rivers.

Shark Attack

Bull sharks will attack and eat almost anything, including people. The large numbers of bull sharks, and the fact that they live near coasts helps explain why they are responsible for so many shark attacks.

Some experts believe that bull sharks are sensitive to low-frequency sounds created by movement in the water. Try not to move if you see one!

Bull sharks often travel in shallow water close to the shore (above), and look very fearsome (below).

Shark attacks on people are actually very rare: Only about 100 attacks are reported around the world each year, and very few of these result in death.

Surfers

Sharks will attack people if they feel threatened or if they mistake someone in the water for prey. Surfers off the coasts of Australia and California are particularly at risk from shark attacks. To a shark, a surfer paddling on a surfboard, with their arms and legs in the water, may look very much like a seal.

A diver wearing chainmail to protect against shark bites.

The shape of a shark's jaw is clearly visible on this man's back.

Eaten

One famous shark attack occurred during World War II. The *USS Indianapolis* was sunk, leaving more than 1,000 men in the water. Rescuers arrived to find only 117 survivors, who reported that their crewmates had all been eaten by sharks!

Electric fence

In places where sharks are common and people spend time in the water, safe areas are enclosed by nets. Experiments have been carried out with a type of electric fence to keep the sharks away from people.

Don't Move

Lifeguards on the beach keep an eye on you and give advice about what to do should you find yourself face to snout with a shark. They recommend remaining as still as possible and punching the shark on the snout to keep them from biting you!

Killer Species

Of the 350 shark species, only 32 are known to have attacked human beings.

Both the board and the surfer were attacked here.

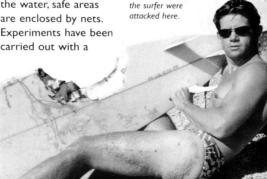

Ampullae of Lorenzini Pores on the side of sharks' heads which pick up electrical signals.

Basking Lying in the sun.

Chainmail Flexible armor made of metal rings or links.

Elasmobranch Family to which sharks, manta rays, skates, guitarfish, and sawfish belong.

Endangered At risk of extinction.

Filter feeders Sea creatures that feed by filtering plankton from the water.

Fossilized Preserved in rock or shell.

Hibernation A long sleep, generally lasting the whole winter.

Luminous Glowing, reflecting, or radiating light.

Migrate Journey to a warmer climate for the winter.

Oviparous Egg-laying sharks.

Ovoviviparous Sharks whose eggs hatch inside the female.

Nocturnal Most active at night.

Plankton Tiny sea creatures and plant material.

Predator A creature that hunts for food.

School A large group of sharks.

Serrated Sawlike.

Species A group of creatures sharing common features.

Spiracle A gill slit.

Streamlined Shaped to move easily through the water.

Temperate Neither too hot, or too cold.

Viviparous Sharks that give birth to live young, called pups.

Acknowledgements

Key: Top - t; middle - m; bottom - b; left - l; right - r; NPL - Naturepl.com; NSP - Natural Science Photos.

Cover: Digital Stock. **1:** Jeff Rotman/npl. **2:** (t) Jeff Rotman/npl; (m) TTAT; (b) Jeff Rotman/NPL. **3:** (t.b) Digital Stock. **4:** (t) Jeff Rotman/NPL; (b) Corel. **5:** (t) Paul Kay/NSP. **6:** Mike Atkinson. **7:** (t) Corel. **8:** (t) Digital Stock; (b) Corel. **9:** Digital Stock. **10:** Brandon Cole/NPL. **11:** (tl) James D. Watt/Seapics.com; (tr) Jeff Rotman/NPL; (bottom: tl,tr,br) Georgette Douwma/Science Photo Library; (bl) Top That!. **12:** (l) Top That!; (r) Steve White. **13:** (tr) Jeff Rotman/NPL; (m,b) Steve White. **14:** (t) Corel; (b) Bob Cranston/NSP. **15:** Digital Stock. **16:** (t) Jeff Rotman NPL; (b) Gary J. Adkison/Seapics.com. **17:** Jeff Rotman/NPL. **18:** Digital Stock. **19:** (t,b) Bob Cranston/NSP; (m) Ken Hoppen/NSP. **20:** Jeff Rotman/NPL. **21:** (t) Bob Cranston/NSP; (m) Top That!; (b) Ben Cropp Productions / Seapics.com. **22:** Jason Isley/Scubazoo.com. **23:** Scott Tuason/imagequest3d.com. **24:** Digital Stock; **25:** (t) James D. Watt/Seapics.com; (b) Bob Cranston/NSP. **26:** (t) Digital Stock; (b) Corel. **27:** (t) Masa Ushioda/Seapics.com; (b) Corel. **28:** (t) Dan Burton/NPL; (b) Jeff Rotman/NPL. **29:** Dan Burton/NPL. **30:** Digital Stock. **31:** Corel. **32:** James D. Watt/Seapics.com. **33:** (t,m) Digital Stock; (b) C&M Fallows/seapics.com. **34:** (t) Alan James/NPL; (b) Paul Kay/NPL. **35:** (t) D P Wilson/FLPA; (b) Paul Kay/NSP. **36:** (t) Bob Cranston/NSP; (b)Jeff Rotman/NPL. **37:** (t) Corel; (b) Francis Abbott/NPL. **38:** (t) Hal Beral/NSP; (b) Hemera. **39:** (t) Hal Beral/FLPA. **40:** John Butler. **41:** Bruce Rasner/ Rotman/NPL **42:** (t) Bob Shanley/Rex Features; (b) Digital Stock. **43:** (t) Masa Ushioda/Imagequest3d.com; (b) Jeff Rotman/NPL. **44:** Brandon Cole/NPL. **45:** (t,b) Jeff Rotman/NPL; (m) Brandon Cole/NPL. **46:** (t) Digital Vision; (b) Corel. **47:** (t) Rex Features; (b) South West News Service/Rex features.